UNICORNS LOVE EASTER

A Creative Colouring Book
Unicolour Books

Printed by Createspace
Available from Amazon.com and other online outlets.

First Printing, 2017

ISBN: 978-1984300942

This Book
Belongs To...

Hello, we would like to thank you for buying our colouring
book. We really hope that you enjoy colouring the
pictures inside this book. If you love this book, we would
love to hear from you. Please feel free to leave us a
review on Amazon.

We would also love to connect with you on Facebook, so
please send us your completed pictures. Our Facebook
page is @Unicolourbooks. Simply search for
@unicolourbooks on Facebook to find our page easily.
Don't forget, we have several books available,
including our best seller 'Unicorns, I Love Them.'
All of our books are available on Amazon
worldwide so please have a look.
Happy colouring!

Unicolour Books

42612510R00038

Made in the USA
Middletown, DE
16 April 2019